MW00333605

INTRODUCTION

The 38 transfer patterns presented here are adapted from *Traditional Chinese Textile Designs* by the Northeast Drama Institute (Dover 0-486-23979-9), a collection of designs taken from Chinese opera costumes.

In traditional Chinese opera, the richly embroidered costumes proclaim the social rank and occupation of the character. Pairs of mandarin ducks, symbols of conjugal bliss, are often used on brides' clothing; the phoenix, representing feminine beauty as well as peace and good fortune, appears on women's robes; and noble creatures such as lions and dragons are used to identify emperors, ministers and other high officials. Cranes symbolize longevity; the lotus, purity; the peony, wealth and honor; plum blossoms, the return of spring; and the bat, through a play on words, stands for happiness.

The originals of these embroideries were worked with fine silk thread. However, silk is expensive, somewhat difficult to work with and not suitable for items subjected to hard wear. The designs are shown here worked with a variety of threads—wool, cotton floss, matte cotton, pearl cotton and cutwork thread.

Satin stitch and its variations were the most commonly used stitches in Chinese embroidery, along with linear stitches such as outline stitch, chain stitch and split stitch. In addition to these traditional stitches, lazy daisy stitch, French knots, straight stitch, fly stitch and back stitch have been used here.

Long and short stitch, a satin stitch variation, is used to blend colors gradually so there is no sharp demarcation line. It is particularly useful for embroidering natural-looking flowers, leaves, birds and animals. When working both regular satin stitch and long and short stitch, angle your stitches to follow the natural curve of the area.

As in the original embroideries, metallic threads have been used to add highlights to the designs. Because these threads are delicate and not as flexible as other threads, they are usually couched in place after the other stitching is complete.

For each project, only one skein of each color listed in the color key is needed unless you are specifically told otherwise. Before beginning a project, study the chart to familiarize yourself with the design. Then read the general directions given with each design and study the stitch details; practice any new stitches on scrap fabric before beginning.

Transfer the design to your fabric following the directions below; carefully read through all directions for transferring before touching iron to paper and fabric! Insert the area to be embroidered in a large hoop, or stretch the fabric on a stretcher frame to keep the work taut. When stapling the fabric to a frame or inserting it in a hoop, try to keep the fabric grain as straight and even as possible to prevent distortion in the finished piece. Embroider the design following the general directions and color and stitch keys. Begin stitching by leaving the end of the yarn or thread on the back of the fabric and working over it to hold it securely. To end a strand or begin a new one, weave the end of the strand under the stitches on the back. Do not make knots. When finished, gently steam-press the embroidery, face down, on a padded surface.

These transfer patterns can be used to make any number of beautiful and unusual gifts and accessories. The larger motifs are suitable for pillows and pictures, or a single large round motif could be embroidered on the back of a jacket to make a one-of-a-kind evening wrap. Small motifs can be used to decorate clothing, pincushions, sachets, pillowcases, placemats, napkins and many other items. The designs can also be used for many craft projects other than the type of embroidery shown here; Russian punchneedle embroidery, fabric painting, woodburning and painting on wood are just some of the possibilities.

Transferring the designs to your fabric is a fairly simple procedure. Here are directions for using these transfer patterns.

A. Prepare the Fabric: If the fabric is washable, preshrink and remove the sizing by laundering first. Iron carefully to remove all wrinkles. If the fabric ravels badly, it is a good idea to whip the edges by hand with an overcast stitch or to run a large zigzag machine stitch along the edges. Since transfers are made with very high temperatures which might melt synthetic fabrics, use a natural fabric such as cotton or linen. If you are unsure of the fibers in your fabric, test the ironability of the fabric first.

B. Prepare the Ironing Board: To prevent the motif from transferring to your ironing board, place an old sheet or other smooth fabric over the ironing board cover. To obtain a stronger impression of the pattern—especially after the transfer has been used, or on darker fabrics—place a piece of aluminum foil on your board before pressing.

C. Make a Test Transfer: Before beginning any project, it is a good idea to test your iron, the fabric and the evenness of your hand pressure. Cut out one of the motifs marked "Test Pattern" and follow the directions below for making a transfer. If the ink transferred well, you can proceed; if not, adjust either the heat or the length of time.

D. Transfer the Patterns:

1. Use a *dry* iron set at medium or wool.

2. Place the fabric on the ironing board, right side up.

3. Cut out the desired motif, allowing a margin around the edges of the design. Pin the design to the fabric with the printed side down. Place the pins through the margins to hold the transfer in place on the fabric. Protect the iron by placing a sheet of tissue paper between the transfer and the iron.

4. Place the heated iron on the transfer and hold down for about 5 seconds. Apply a firm, downward even pressure to all parts of the design, being especially careful to get the outer edges, such as the tips of leaves and flowers. Do not move the iron back and forth across the fabric as this will cause the transfer pattern to blur. After the transfer has been used once, add 2–3 seconds to the pressing time for each additional transfer.

5. Carefully remove one pin and lift one side of the transfer paper to see whether the complete design is indicated on the fabric. If not, replace the pin and repeat the process, concentrating on the area that did not transfer. Do not remove all the pins until you are sure the design has been successfully transferred. Once the pattern has been unpinned, it is almost impossible to register it to the fabric again.

6. When you are satisfied that the transferring has been completed, unpin the transfer paper and peel it off. You will want to save the transfer paper to use for additional repeats (you can usually get four or more transfers from each pattern) or to use as a check on the design. If the design is not clear enough, you can refer to the transfer sheet and reinforce vague areas on the fabric with a waterproof felt pen or laundry marker. Make sure that the ink is completely waterproof because just the moisture from a steam iron can cause the ink to run and ruin your embroidery.

E. Special Instructions for Use on Dark Fabrics: If you wish to use these patterns on dark fabric on which transfer ink will not show up, or if you need additional repeats of the same transfer, put a piece of tracing paper over the uninked side of the transfer and trace the design. Discard the original transfer paper and pin the tracing in place on the fabric. Slip a piece of dressmaker's carbon, color-side down, between the fabric and the tracing; do not pin the carbon. With a hard, even pressure, trace a few lines with a tracing wheel, stylus or similar tool. Raise one corner of the tracing and the carbon to check the impression. If the results are too faint, apply more pressure; if too heavy, less pressure. After adjusting the impression, trace the entire design and then remove the carbon and carefully remove one pin to see whether the design is intact on the fabric *before removing the pattern.*

IMPORTANT

Since these transfer patterns are made to be used more than once, the ink will not readily wash out of the fabric. It is therefore important that the embroidery cover all transfer markings.

Dover Publications assumes no responsibility for any damage to fabrics caused by the transfer inks in this book.

STITCH DETAILS

SATIN STITCH (A)

LONG AND SHORT STITCH (B)

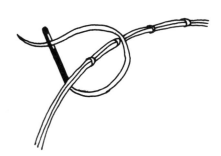

COUCHING (C)

OUTLINE STITCH (D)

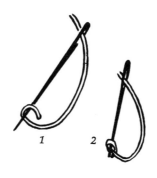

FRENCH KNOT (E)

SPLIT STITCH (F)

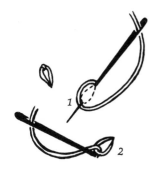

LAZY DAISY STITCH (G)

STRAIGHT STITCH (H)

CHAIN STITCH (J)

PADDED SATIN STITCH (K)

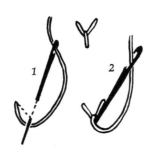

FLY STITCH (L)

BACK STITCH (M)

Stitch and Color Chart for Plate 1, PHOENIX

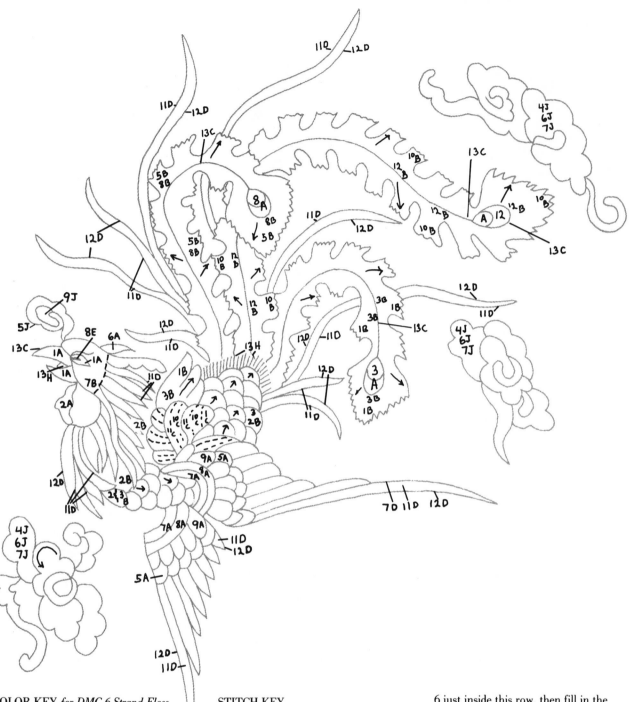

COLOR KEY *for DMC 6-Strand Floss*

1 Light Topaz (726)
2 Light Melon (3341)
3 Medium Coral (350)
4 White
5 Light Terra-Cotta (758)
6 Very Light Blue (827)
7 Very Dark Blue (824)
8 Dark Coffee Brown (801)
9 Medium Terra-Cotta (356)
10 Very Light Loden Green (772)
11 Light Parrot Green (907)
12 Medium Emerald Green (911)
13 DMC Gold Embroidery Thread, Art. 282

STITCH KEY

A Satin Stitch
B Long and Short Stitch
C Couching
D Outline Stitch
E French Knot
H Straight Stitch
J Chain Stitch

DIRECTIONS

Work with three strands of floss in needle. Clouds are worked in chain stitch as follows: Outline the outer edge of each section with color 4. Work a row of color 6 just inside this row, then fill in the center with color 7. Work long, thin head and wing feathers in outline stitch, using color 12 on the lower edge of each feather and color 11 on the upper edge. Work long, thin tail feathers in outline stitch, using color 12 on the right edge of each feather, color 11 in the center and color 7 on the left edge. Work the body in long and short stitch with colors 2 and 3. After all other stitching has been completed, outline head, beak, eye, body and feathers of bird and work center spines of tail feathers in couching with one strand of color 13.

Stitch and Color Chart for Plate 2, CHRYSANTHEMUMS

COLOR KEY *for DMC 3-Ply Persian Wool*

1 Light Pumpkin (7941)
2 Bright Orange Red (7606)
3 Dark Red Copper (7110)
4 Dark Mauve (7259)
5 DMC Gold Embroidery Thread, Art. 282

STITCH KEY

A Satin Stitch
C Couching
D Outline Stitch

DIRECTIONS

Work with one strand of yarn in needle. Work top and bottom flowers with color 2, center flower with color 1. Work stems in outline stitch and calyxes in satin stitch with color 4. After all other stitching has been completed, outline petals, buds and stems and work veins in leaves in couching with one strand of color 5.

Stitch and Color Chart for Plate 3, GOLDFISH

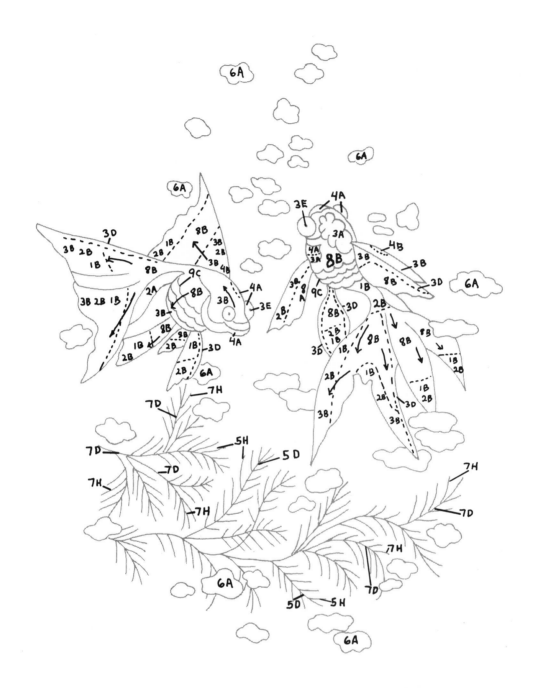

COLOR KEY *for DMC 6-Strand Floss.*

1 Light Peach (754)
2 Coral (351)
3 Bright Christmas Red (666)
4 Dark Garnet Red (814)
5 Dark Emerald Green (910)
6 Aquamarine (992)
7 Light Aquamarine (993)
8 Off White (746)
9 DMC Gold Embroidery Thread, Art. 282

STITCH KEY

A Satin Stitch
B Long and Short Stitch
C Couching
D Outline Stitch
E French Knot
H Straight Stitch

DIRECTIONS

Work with three strands of floss in needle. Work "bubbles" in satin stitch with color 6. Work the plants in outline stitch and straight stitch, working unmarked sections with color 5. After all other stitching has been completed, outline the fish in couching with one strand of color 9.

Stitch and Color Chart for Plate 4, LION PLAYING WITH A BALL

COLOR KEY *for DMC 3-Ply Persian Wool*

1 Black (three skeins needed)
2 DMC Gold Embroidery Thread, Art. 282

STITCH KEY

A Satin Stitch
B Long and Short Stitch
C Couchïng
D Outline Stitch
E French Knot (wrap yarn around needle twice)
J Chain Stitch

DIRECTIONS

Work with one strand of yarn in needle. Work entire piece with color 1 unless otherwise indicated. Fill in eyes with chain stitch using one strand of color 2 and following direction of arrows. After all other stitching has been completed, work couching with one strand of color 2 as indicated.

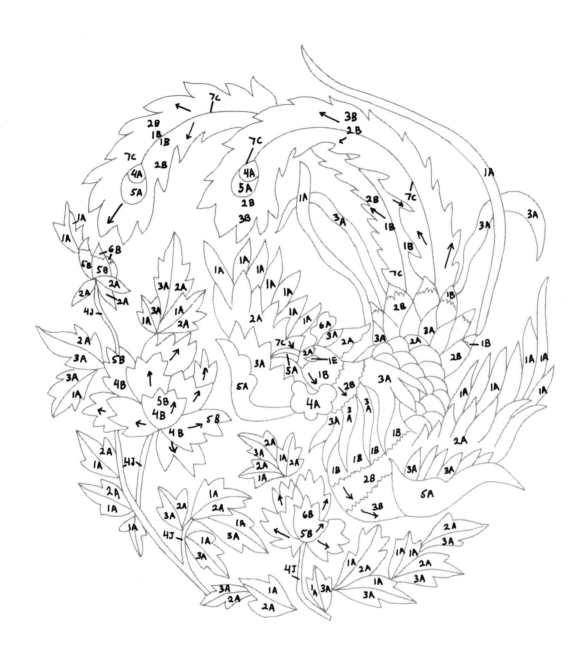

COLOR KEY *for DMC 3-Ply Persian Wool*

1 Royal Blue (7797—2 skeins needed)
2 Light Electric Blue (7997)
3 Light Turquoise (7699)
4 Strawberry (7107)
5 Medium Carnation Pink (7893)
6 Light Carnation Pink (7103)
7 DMC Silver Metallic Thread, Art. 281

STITCH KEY

A Satin Stitch
B Long and Short Stitch
C Couching
E French Knot
J Chain Stitch

DIRECTIONS

Work with one strand of yarn in needle. After all other stitching has been completed, work center spine of tail feathers and veins of leaves in couching with a single strand of color 7. Outline bird's head, eye, body and feathers in couching with one strand of color 7.

Stitch and Color Chart for Plate 6, CHRYSANTHEMUM

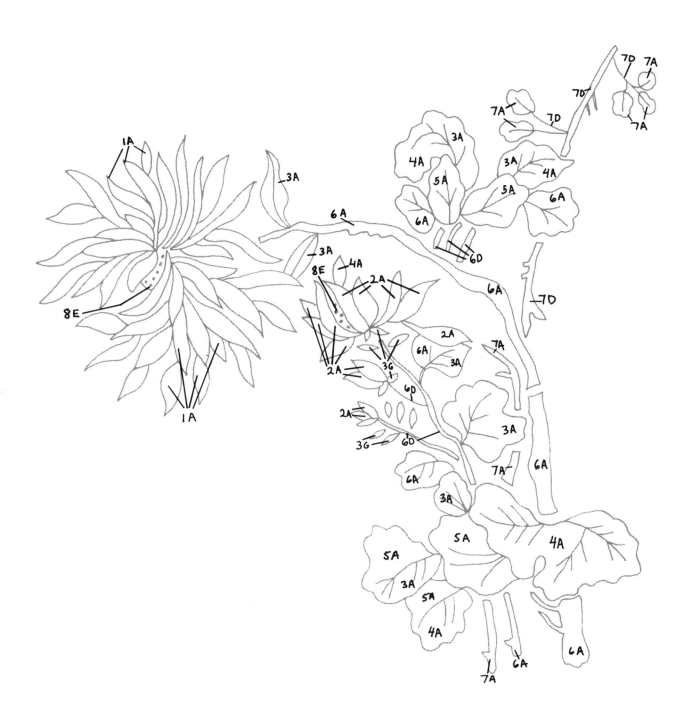

COLOR KEY *for DMC Matte Embroidery Cotton*

1 Light Yellow (2745)
2 Dark Yellow (2743)
3 Very Dark Emerald Green (2909)
4 Very Dark Blue Green (2500)
5 Avocado Green (2469)
6 Medium Avocado Green (2937)
7 Dark Red Copper (2918)
8 DMC Gold Embroidery Thread, Art. 282

STITCH KEY

A Satin Stitch
C Couching
D Outline Stitch
E French Knot
G Lazy Daisy Stitch
H Straight Stitch

DIRECTIONS

Work with one strand of thread in needle. Work the petals of the large flower with color 1, the petals of the small flower with color 2. After all other stitching has been completed, outline petals and work veins in leaves in couching with two strands of color 8.

Stitch and Color Chart for Plate 7, PHOENIX AND FLOWERS

COLOR KEY *for DMC 3-Ply Persian Wool*

1 Spice Brown (7166)
2 White
3 Light Aqua (7559)
4 Aqua (7806)
5 Light Sea Foam Green (7952)
6 Dark Parrot Green (7904)
7 Light Lilac (7795)
8 Dark Lilac (7478)
9 Light Topaz (7726)
10 Light Geranium Pink (7104)
11 Dark Geranium Pink (7566)
12 Strawberry (7107)
13 Light Parrot Green (7907)
14 DMC Silver Metallic Thread, Art. 281

STITCH KEY

A Satin Stitch
B Long and Short Stitch
C Couching
H Straight Stitch
K Padded Satin Stitch

DIRECTIONS

Work with one strand of yarn in needle. Embroider unmarked leaves in satin stitch, working half of leaf with color 2 and half with color 5. Work unmarked feathers in long and short stitch with colors 2 and 4. After all other stitching has been completed, outline petals of flowers, bird's feathers, beak and eye and work veins in leaves in couching with one strand of color 14.

Stitch and Color Chart for Plate 8, LONGEVITY

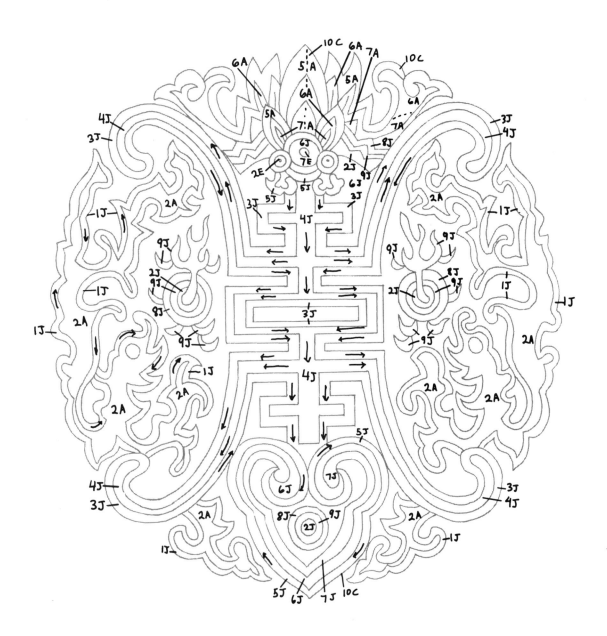

COLOR KEY *for DMC Matte Embroidery Cotton*

1 Light Beige Brown (2841)
2 Black (2310)
3 Peacock Blue (2807)
4 Dark Peacock Blue (2592)
5 Very Light Antique Blue (2933)
6 Light Antique Blue (2932)
7 Very Dark Antique Blue (2929)
8 Dark Lemon Yellow (2444)
9 Medium Coral (2350)
10 DMC Silver Embroidery Thread, Art. 283

STITCH KEY

A Satin Stitch
C Couching
E French Knot
J Chain Stitch

DIRECTIONS

Work with one strand of thread in needle. Work the center and lower symbols in chain stitch following the direction of the arrows. Work the side sections in satin stitch, then outline with chain stitch. After all other stitching has been completed, outline the top and bottom symbols in couching with one strand of color 10.

13

Stitch and Color Chart for Plate 9, FIVE BLESSINGS AND LONG LIFE

COLOR KEY *for DMC Pearl Cotton #5*

1 Black (310)
2 White
3 Dark Garnet Red (814)
4 Dark Steel Gray (414)
5 Pearl Gray (415)
6 DMC Gold Embroidery Thread, Art. 282

STITCH KEY

A Satin Stitch
B Long and Short Stitch
C Couching
J Chain Stitch

DIRECTIONS

Work with one strand of pearl cotton or metallic thread in needle. Fill center motif with chain stitch, using color 6 and following direction of arrows. Work satin stitch and long and short stitch in border as indicated. After all other stitching has been completed, outline outer edge and small gray and white motifs in couching with color 5. Outline garnet red motifs in couching with color 6.

14

Stitch and Color Chart for Plate 10, PHOENIX

COLOR KEY *for DMC 6-Strand Floss*

1 Light Navy Blue (312)
2 White
3 Bright Orange Red (606)
4 Medium Electric Blue (996)
5 Dark Sea Foam Green (561)
6 Very Light Loden Green (772)
7 Light Coral (352)
8 Very Light Peach (948)
9 Peach (353)
10 Medium Bittersweet (722)
11 Medium Navy Blue (311)
12 Light Lavender (211)
13 Light Baby Blue (775)
14 Pale Pistachio Green (369)
15 Medium Nile Green (913)
16 DMC Gold Embroidery Thread, Art. 282

STITCH KEY

A Satin Stitch
B Long and Short Stitch
C Couching
D Outline Stitch
E French Knot
G Lazy Daisy Stitch
J Chain Stitch
L Fly Stitch

DIRECTIONS

Work with three strands of floss in needle. Work tail and wing feathers in long and short stitch, following the direction of the arrows and shading as shown. Work flower at lower left in long and short stitch, shading each petal from color 3 at center to color 9 at outer edge. To work the area marked "3A & 9L," first fill the area with satin stitch, then work fly stitches over the satin stitch. After all other stitching has been completed, outline the head, beak, eye and body in couching with one strand of color 16. Use one strand of color 16 to couch center spine and around "eye" of each tail feather.

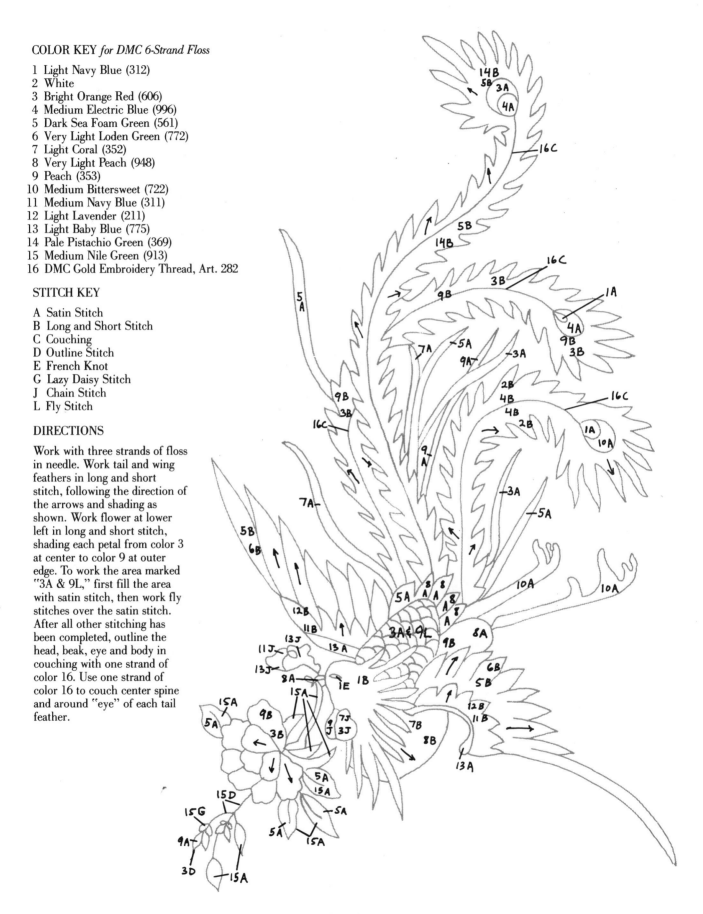

15

Stitch and Color Chart for Plate 11, TWO LIONS PLAYING WITH A BALL

COLOR KEY *for DMC 3-Ply Persian Wool*

1 Dark Peacock Blue (7607)
2 Dark Cranberry (7601)
3 Very Light Cranberry (7605)
4 Medium Carnation Pink (7893)
5 Black
6 White
7 Dark Parrot Green (7904)
8 Christmas Green (7346)
9 Medium Lemon Yellow (7019)
10 Christmas Gold (7473)
11 Light Gray Blue (7928)
12 DMC Gold Embroidery Thread, Art. 282

STITCH KEY

A Satin Stitch
B Long and Short Stitch
C Couching
F Split Stitch
G Lazy Daisy Stitch
H Straight Stitch
J Chain Stitch

DIRECTIONS

Work with one strand of yarn in needle.
Fill small circles around lions' heads and at end of tail with chain stitch using color 7; outline in couching with color 12. Fill ball with chain stitch using color 12. After all other stitching has been completed, outline mane and tail in split stitch with color 10, then in couching with color 12. Outline lions' feet and heads and faces in couching with color 12 as indicated by black lines.

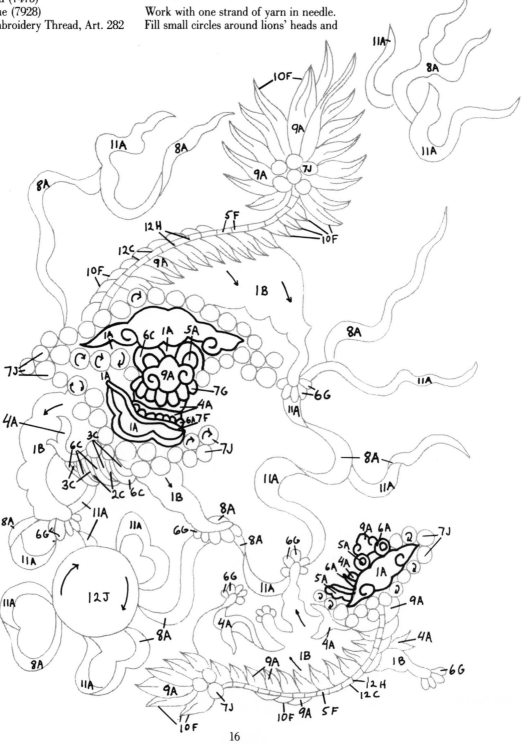

16

Phoenix

Test Pattern

Plate 1

Chrysanthemums

Test Pattern

Plate 2

Test Pattern

Goldfish

Plate 3

Lion Playing with a Ball

Test Pattern

Plate 4

Phoenix

Test Pattern

Plate 5

Chrysanthemum

Test Pattern

Plate 6

Phoenix and Flowers

Test Pattern

Plate 7

Test Pattern

Longevity

Plate 8

Test Pattern

Five Blessings and Long Life

Plate 9

Test Pattern

Phoenix

Plate 10

Two Lions Playing with a Ball

Test Pattern

Plate 11

Test Pattern

Mandarin Ducks and Lotus

Plate 12

Test Pattern

Peony

Plate 13

Plate 13

Test Pattern

Dragon

Plate 14

Test Pattern

Lotus

Plate 15

Crane

Test Pattern

Plate 16

Test Pattern

Crane

Plate 17

Test Pattern

Pear Blossoms

Chrysanthemums

Plate 18

Peony

Fish

Peony and Plum Blossoms

Chrysanthemum

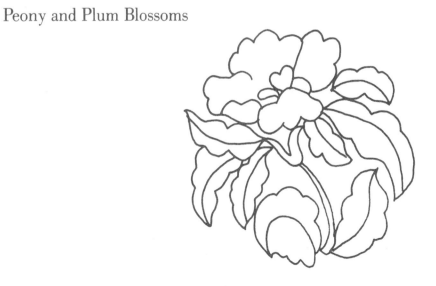

Camellia

Plate 19

Pear Blossoms

Apricot Blossoms

Plate 20

Pink Chrysanthemums

Violet Chrysanthemums

Plate 21

Wisteria

Cranes

Peony

Day Lilies

Test Pattern

Plate 22

Orange and Red Butterfly

Red and Green Butterfly

Peony

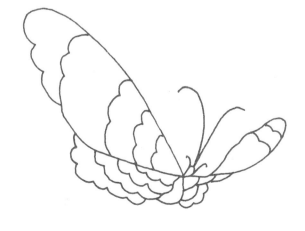

Green Butterfly

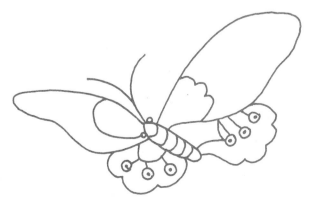

Pink and Yellow Butterfly

Plate 23

Two Phoenixes

Test Pattern

Plate 24

Stitch and Color Chart for Plate 12, MANDARIN DUCKS AND LOTUS

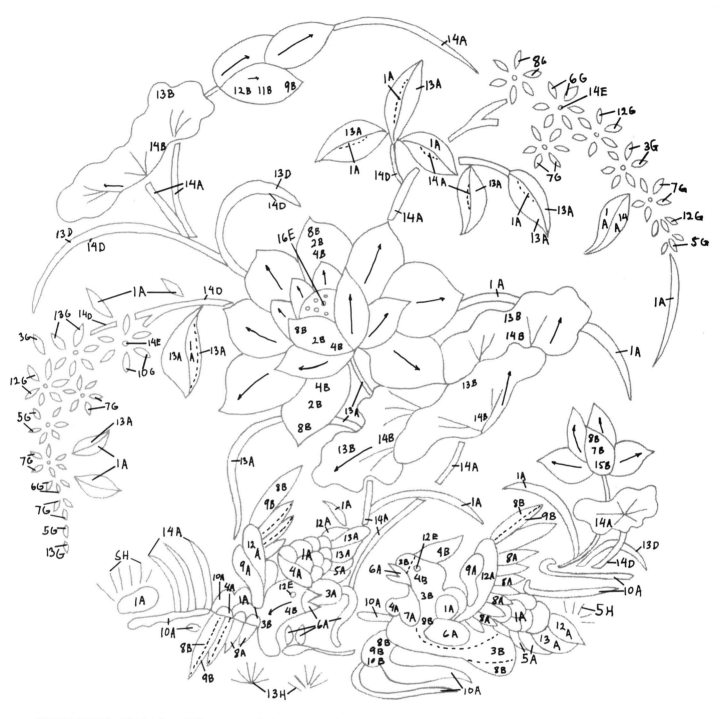

COLOR KEY *for DMC 6-Strand Floss*

1 Very Dark Pistachio Green (319)
2 Medium Pink (776)
3 Light Rose (3326)
4 Deep Rose (309)
5 Lemon Yellow (307)
6 Light Tangerine (742)
7 Pumpkin (971)
8 White
9 Very Pale Blue (828)
10 Light Blue (813)
11 Medium Blue (826)
12 Very Dark Blue (824)
13 Light Pistachio Green (368)
14 Medium Pistachio Green (320)
15 Dark Burnt Orange (900)
16 DMC Gold Embroidery Thread, Árt. 282

STITCH KEY

A Satin Stitch
B Long and Short Stitch
C Couching
D Outline Stitch
E French Knot
G Lazy Daisy Stitch
H Straight Stitch

DIRECTIONS

Work with three strands of floss in needle. Each flower is worked in long and short stitch, shading the petals from dark at the center to light at the outer edge. After all other stitching has been completed, work veins in large leaves in straight stitch with color 1. Work center vein in small leaves and outline petals of flowers and each section of ducks in couching with one strand of color 16.

17

Stitch and Color Chart for Plate 13, PEONY

COLOR KEY *for DMC Matte Embroidery Cotton*

1 Medium Garnet Red (2815)
2 Bright Christmas Red (2666)
3 Coral (2351)
4 White
5 Very Light Avocado Green (2472)
6 Light Avocado Green (2471)
7 Medium Light Avocado Green (2470)

8 Medium Avocado Green (2937)
9 DMC Gold Embroidery Thread,
  Art. 282

STITCH KEY

A Satin Stitch
B Long and Short Stitch
J Chain Stitch

DIRECTIONS

Work with one strand of thread in
needle. Fill triangles around edge of
design with rows of chain stitch using
one strand of color 9. Each petal of
flower is shaded from color 4 on the
outside edge to color 1 on the inside.
Where there is not enough room for all
four colors, omit the darker colors.

18

Stitch and Color Chart for Plate 14, DRAGON

COLOR KEY *for DMC 3-Ply Persian Wool*

1 White
2 Light Steel Gray (7618)
3 Black
4 Coral (7851)
5 Dark Coral (7891)
6 Chartreuse (7342)
7 Christmas Green (7346)
8 Light Electric Blue (7997)
9 Dark Electric Blue (7995)
10 DMC Silver Metallic Thread, Art. 281

STITCH KEY

A Satin Stitch
B Long and Short Stitch
C Couching
E French Knot (wrap yarn around needle twice)
L Fly Stitch

DIRECTIONS

Work with one strand of yarn in needle.
Work dragon's scales as follows: Work
center of each scale in satin stitch with
color 4; with color 9, work a fly stitch
around this center, then work couching
around the fly stitch with color 8. After
all other stitching has been completed,
outline all white areas and outer edge of
all gray areas in couching with one strand
of color 10. Outline dragon's head in
couching with color 10.

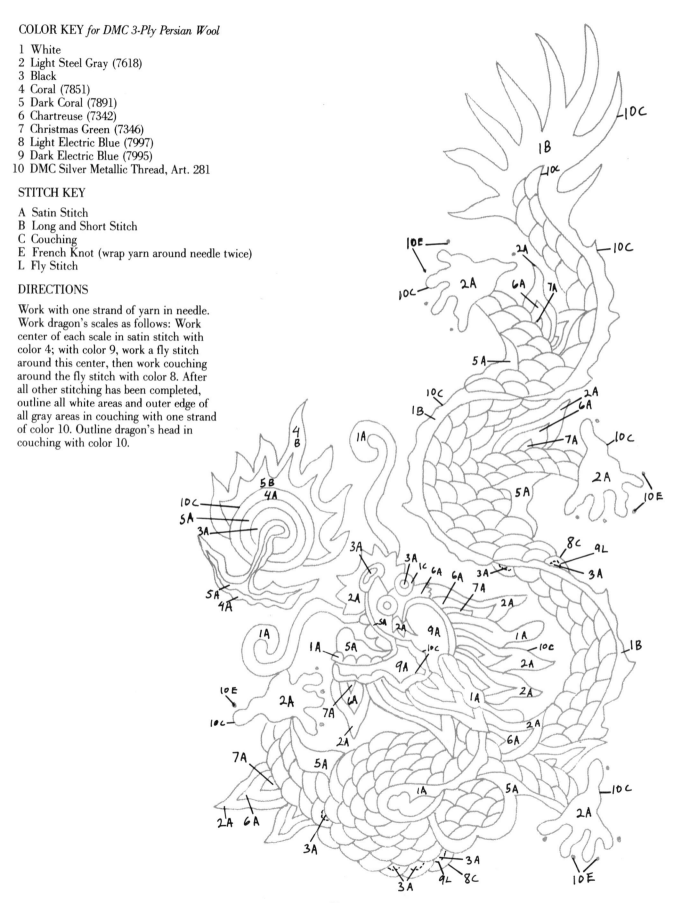

Stitch and Color Chart for Plate 15, LOTUS

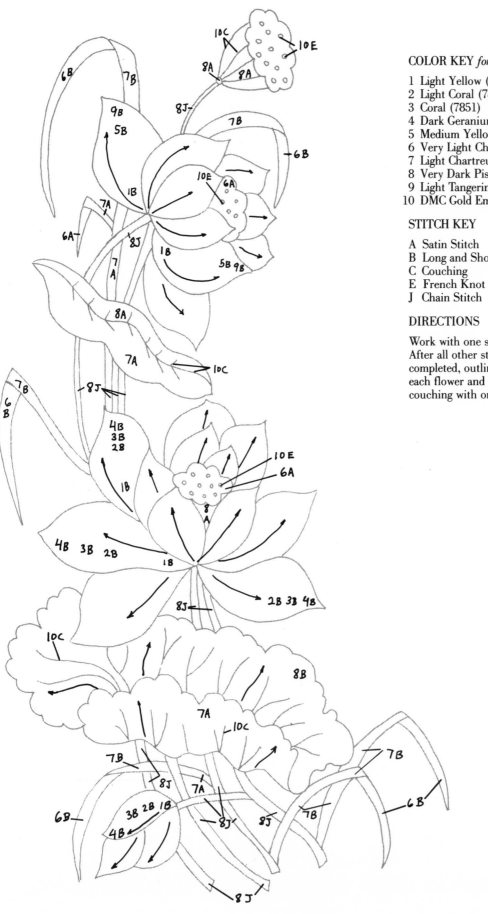

COLOR KEY *for DMC 3-Ply Persian Wool*

1 Light Yellow (7745)
2 Light Coral (7852)
3 Coral (7851)
4 Dark Geranium Pink (7566)
5 Medium Yellow (7744)
6 Very Light Chartreuse (7113)
7 Light Chartreuse (7341)
8 Very Dark Pistachio Green (7541)
9 Light Tangerine (7742)
10 DMC Gold Embroidery Thread, Art. 282

STITCH KEY

A Satin Stitch
B Long and Short Stitch
C Couching
E French Knot (wrap yarn around needle twice)
J Chain Stitch

DIRECTIONS

Work with one strand of yarn in needle.
After all other stitching has been
completed, outline petals and center of
each flower and work veins in leaves in
couching with one strand of color 10.

Stitch and Color Chart for Plate 16, CRANE

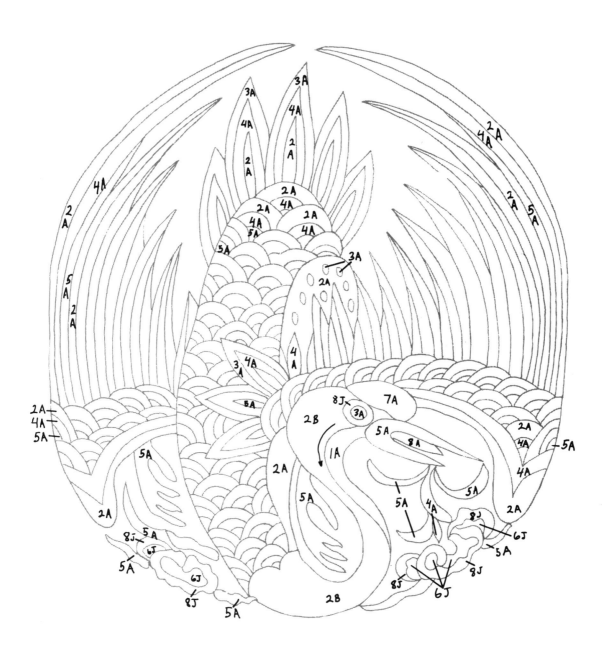

COLOR KEY *for DMC 3-Ply Persian Wool*

1 Medium Dark Ash Gray (7877)
2 White (2 skeins needed)
3 Black
4 Medium Jade Green (7956—
   2 skeins needed)
5 Christmas Green (7346)
6 Bright Gold (7040)
7 Dark Geranium Pink (7566)
8 Bright Canary Yellow (7973)
9 DMC Silver Metallic Thread, Art. 281

STITCH KEY

A Satin Stitch
B Long and Short Stitch
C Couching
E French Knot
J Chain Stitch

DIRECTIONS

Work with one strand of yarn in needle.
All feathers are worked in satin stitch.
Work long, thin upright feathers as

follows: Starting with outside feather on each side, work first, then every third feather with color 2, work second, then every third feather with color 4 and remaining feathers with color 5. Working from outer edge to center, work each scalloped feather in color 2, color 4 and color 5, each larger feather at tail and back of head in color 3, color 4 and color 2. After all other stitching has been completed, outline head, beak, eye, neck and black rim of feathers in couching with color 9.

Stitch and Color Chart for Plate 17, CRANE

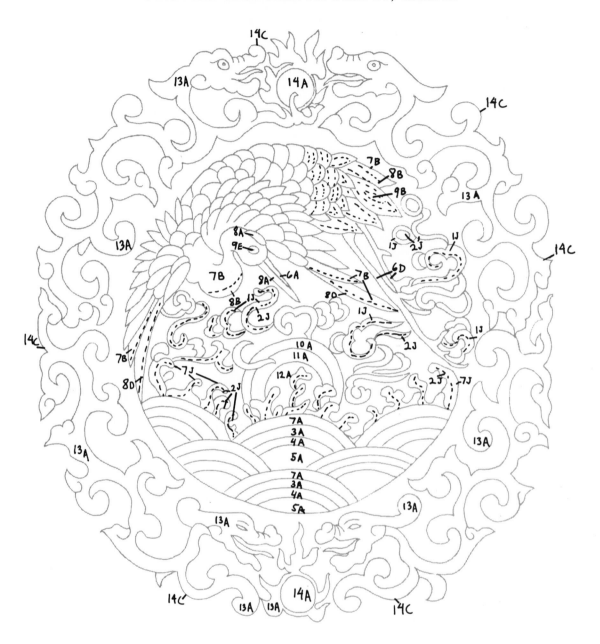

COLOR KEY *for DMC 3-Ply Persian Wool*

1 Light Baby Blue (7775)
2 Dark Electric Blue (7995)
3 Pale Pistachio Green (7604)
4 Medium Pistachio Green (7542)
5 Very Dark Pistachio Green (7540)
6 Yellow Orange (7972)
7 White
8 Light Ash Gray (7380)
9 Dark Beaver Gray (7844)
10 Baby Pink (7818)
11 Light Cranberry (7804)
12 Dark Carnation (7106)
13 Light Red Brown (7873—
    2 skeins needed)

14 Medium Burnt Orange (7946)
15 DMC Gold Embroidery Thread,
   Art. 282

STITCH KEY

A Satin Stitch
B Long and Short Stitch
C Couching
D Outline Stitch
E French Knot
J Chain Stitch

DIRECTIONS

Work with one strand of yarn in needle. Work outer "frame" in satin stitch with color 13, outline in couching with color

14. Work hills in satin stitch with colors 7, 3, 4 and 5 as indicated. Work ocean waves in chain stitch, using color 7 on outer edge of each wave and color 2 on inner edge. Work clouds in chain stitch, using color 1 on outer edge of each cloud and color 2 on inner edge. Working from the center of each feather to the outer edge, work feathers on crane's body in long and short stitch with colors 9, 8 and 7. Work wing feathers in long and short stitch with color 7, work a row of outline stitch with color 8 along lower edge of each feather. After all other stitching has been completed, outline hills, sun and crane's body, feathers, eye and bill in couching with color 15.

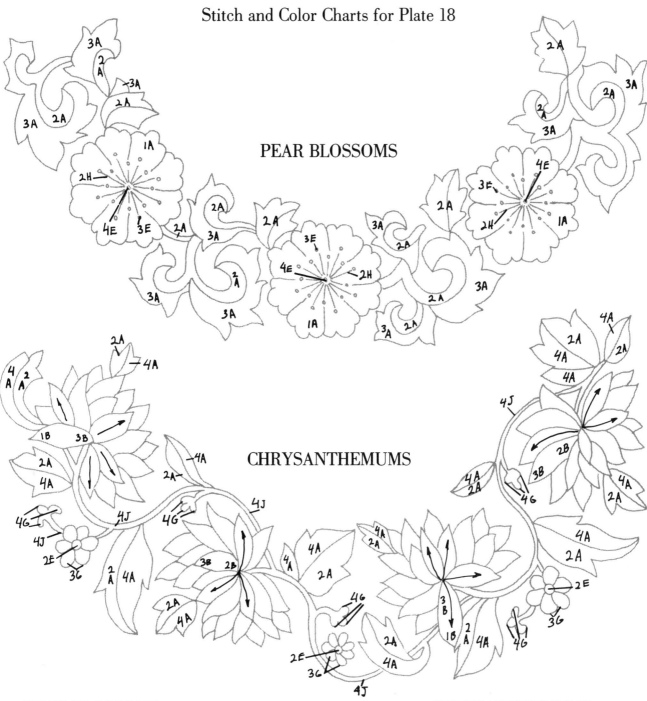

PEAR BLOSSOMS

CHRYSANTHEMUMS

PEAR BLOSSOMS

COLOR KEY *for DMC Pearl Cotton #5*

1 Medium Electric Blue (996)
2 Light Parrot Green (907)
3 Christmas Green (699)
4 DMC Gold Metallic Thread, Art 280

DIRECTIONS

Work with one strand of thread in needle. After all other stitching has been completed, outline petals and work veins in leaves in couching with one strand of color 4. Wrapping the thread around the needle four times, work a French knot at the center of each flower with color 4.

STITCH KEY for Both Designs

A Satin Stitch
B Long and Short Stitch
C Couching
E French Knot
G Lazy Daisy Stitch
H Straight Stitch
J Chain Stitch

CHRYSANTHEMUMS

COLOR KEY *for DMC 3-Ply Persian Wool*

1 White
2 Dark Electric Blue (7995)
3 Peacock Blue (7608)
4 Dark Jade Green (7093)
5 DMC Gold Embroidery Thread, Art. 282

DIRECTIONS

Work with one strand of yarn in needle. After all other stitching has been completed, outline petals and work veins in leaves in couching with one strand of color 5.

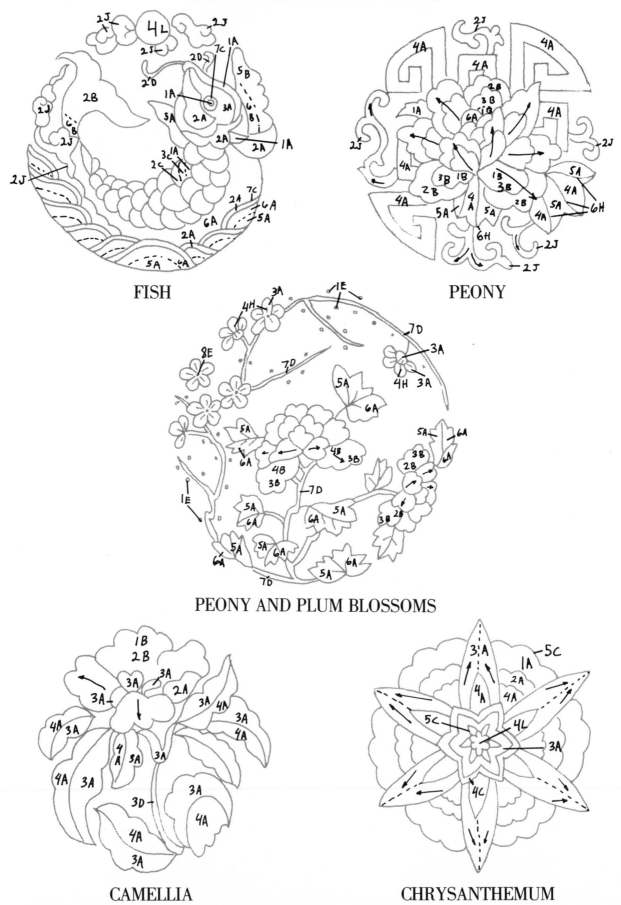

FISH

PEONY

PEONY AND PLUM BLOSSOMS

CAMELLIA

CHRYSANTHEMUM

FISH

COLOR KEY *for DMC 6-Strand Floss*

1 Black (310)
2 White
3 Dark Steel Gray (414)
4 Bright Orange Red (606)
5 Dark Emerald Green (910)
6 Medium Nile Green (913)
7 DMC Silver Metallic Thread, Art. 281

DIRECTIONS

Work with three strands of floss in needle. To work inner scales, fill the center of each scale with satin stitch with color 1; couch 2 rows of color 3 and one row of color 2 around the center. When all other stitching has been completed, outline the tail, head, eye and large scales on the back and the circle at the top in couching with color 7.

STITCH KEY for All Designs

A Satin Stitch
B Long and Short Stitch
C Couching
D Outline Stitch
E French Knot
H Straight Stitch
J Chain Stitch
K Padded Satin Stitch

CAMELLIA

COLOR KEY *for DMC 3-Ply Persian Wool*

1 Lemon Yellow (7971)
2 Light Pumpkin (7436)
3 Medium Coral (7892)
4 Dark Old Rose (7210)
5 DMC Gold Embroidery Thread, Art. 282

DIRECTIONS

Work with one strand of yarn in needle. Work flower in long and short stitch, shading each petal from dark at center to light at edge. After all other stitching has been completed, outline center of flower and petals and work veins of leaves in couching with one strand of color 5.

PEONY

COLOR KEY *for DMC Pearl Cotton #5*

1 Coral (351)
2 White
3 Dark Beige Gray (642)
4 Medium Garnet Red (815)
5 Tan (436)
6 DMC Gold Embroidery Thread, Art. 282

DIRECTIONS

Work with one strand of thread in needle. Work flower in long and short stitch, shading each petal as shown. After all other stitching has been completed, work straight stitches on leaves with one strand of color 6.

PEONY AND PLUM BLOSSOMS

COLOR KEY *for DMC Cutwork Thread, size #16*

1 Peach (353)
2 Medium Burnt Orange (946)
3 White
4 Rose (335)
5 Bright Chartreuse (704)
6 Light Parrot Green (907)
7 Very Dark Garnet Red (902)
8 DMC Gold Metallic Thread, Art. 282

DIRECTIONS

Work with two strands of thread in needle. Work larger flowers in long and short stitch, shading each petal from dark at the center to light at the edge. After all other stitching has been completed, work veins of leaves in couching with color 8. When working French knots, wrap the thread around the needle twice.

CHRYSANTHEMUM

COLOR KEY *for DMC Matte Embroidery Cotton*

1 Light Yellow (2745)
2 Very Light Terra-Cotta (2759)
3 Medium Tangerine (2741)
4 Medium Coral (2350)
5 DMC Gold Metallic Thread, Art. 280

DIRECTIONS

Work with one strand of thread in needle. After all other stitching has been completed, couch outlines with one strand of color 5.

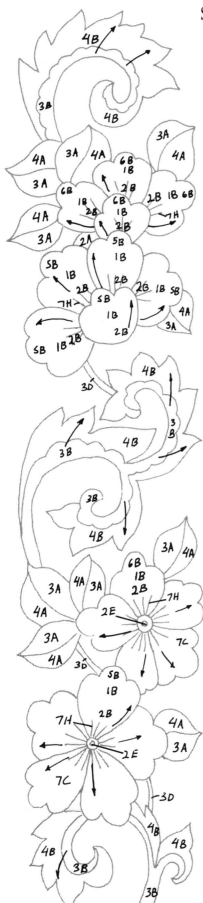

PEAR BLOSSOMS

COLOR KEY *for DMC 3-Ply Persian Wool*

1 Light Turquoise (7699)
2 Turquoise (7597)
3 Dark Emerald Green (7009)
4 Chartreuse (7342)
5 Very Light Almond Green (7400)
6 White
7 DMC Gold Embroidery Thread, Art. 282

DIRECTIONS

Work with one strand of yarn in needle.
After all other stitching has been
completed, outline flowers and work
veins in leaves in couching with one
strand of color 7. Work straight stitches
at center of each flower with one strand
of color 7.

STITCH KEY for Both Designs

A Satin Stitch
B Long and Short Stitch
C Couching
D Outline Stitch
E French Knot (wrap yarn around
   needle twice)
H Straight Stitch

APRICOT BLOSSOMS

COLOR KEY *for DMC Pearl Cotton #5*

1 White
2 Bright Christmas Red (666)
3 Christmas Green (699)
4 Medium Pink (776)
5 Very Dark Parrot Green (905)
6 DMC Gold Metallic Thread, Art. 280

DIRECTIONS

Work with one strand of thread in
needle. Fill center of each flower with
several French knots, using one strand of
color 6. After all other stitching has been
completed, outline flowers and work
veins in leaves in couching with one
strand of color 6. Work straight stitches
at center of each flower with one strand
of color 6.

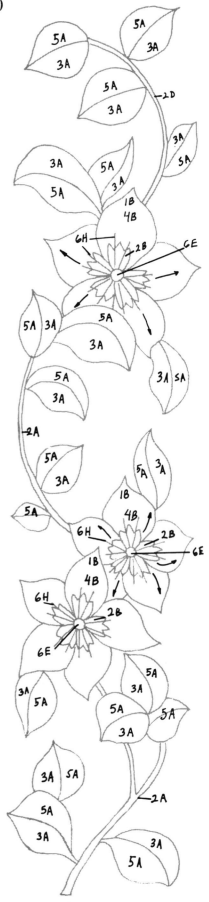

PEAR BLOSSOMS

APRICOT BLOSSOMS

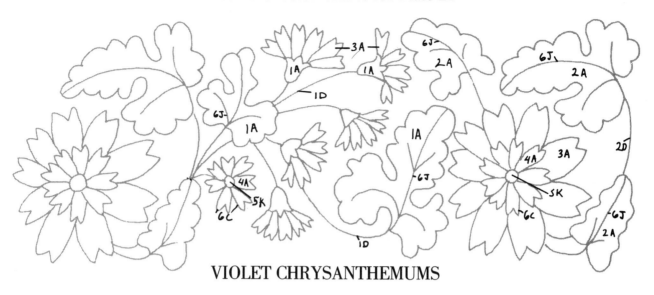

VIOLET CHRYSANTHEMUMS

VIOLET CHRYSANTHEMUMS

COLOR KEY *for DMC 3-Ply Persian Wool*

1 Black
2 Light Lilac (7795)
3 Light Yellow (7745)
4 Bright Canary Yellow (7973)
5 Bright Christmas Red (7666)
6 DMC Silver Embroidery Thread, Art. 283

DIRECTIONS

Work with one strand of yarn in needle.
Only one and a half repeats of the design
are shown. After all other stitching has
been completed, work veins in leaves in
chain stitch and outline centers of
flowers in couching with one strand of
color 6.

STITCH KEY for Both Designs

A Satin Stitch
C Couching
D Outline Stitch
J Chain Stitch
K Padded Satin Stitch
M Back Stitch

PINK CHRYSANTHEMUMS

COLOR KEY *for DMC Matte Embroidery Cotton*

1 Very Dark Mauve (2497)
2 Bright Christmas Red (2666)
3 Deep Rose (2309)
4 DMC Gold Embroidery Thread, Art. 282

DIRECTIONS

Work with one strand of thread in
needle. Only one and a half repeats of the
design are shown. Work all leaves in satin
stitch with color 1.

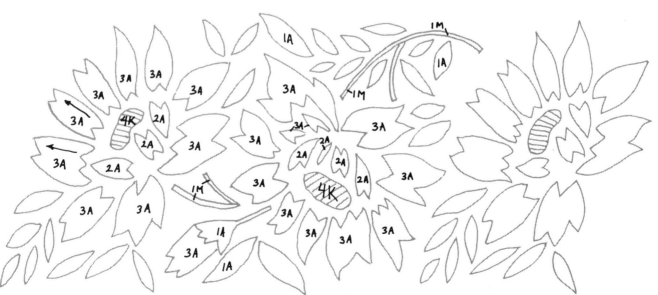

PINK CHRYSANTHEMUMS

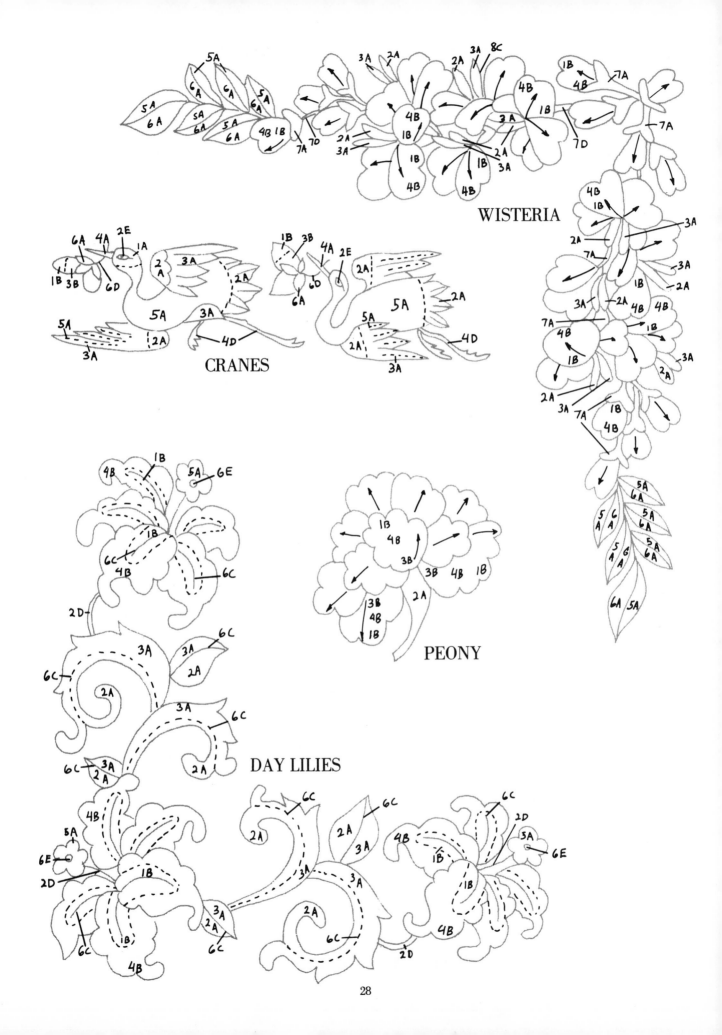

WISTERIA

CRANES

DAY LILIES

PEONY

28

CRANES

COLOR KEY *for DMC 6-Strand Floss*

1 Bright Orange Red (606)
2 Black (310)
3 White
4 Tangerine (740)
5 Light Steel Gray (318)
6 Light Christmas Green (701)
7 DMC Silver Embroidery Thread, Art. 283

DIRECTIONS

Work with three strands of floss in
needle. After all other stitching has been
completed, outline leaves, beaks and
black portions of feathers in couching
with color 7.

STITCH KEY for All Designs

A Satin Stitch
B Long and Short Stitch
C Couching
D Outline Stitch
E French Knot
H Straight Stitch

DAY LILIES

COLOR KEY *for DMC Cutwork Thread, size 12*

1 Burnt Orange (947)
2 Medium Garnet Red (815)
3 Dark Burnt Orange (900)
4 Tangerine (740)
5 Bright Christmas Red (666)
6 DMC Gold Embroidery Thread, Art. 282

DIRECTIONS

Work with two strands of thread in
needle. After all other stitching has been
completed, work couching as indicated,
using one strand of color 6. When
working French knots, wrap yarn around
needle twice.

WISTERIA

COLOR KEY *for DMC 3-Ply Persian Wool*

1 Light Purple (7554)
2 Medium Purple (7553)
3 Very Dark Purple (7550)
4 White
5 Light Parrot Green (7907)
6 Light Sea Foam Green (7564)
7 Pale Pistachio Green (7604)
8 DMC Gold Embroidery Thread, Art. 282

DIRECTIONS

Work with one strand of yarn in needle.
Work petals and buds in long and short
stitch, shading each petal from dark at
the center to light at the outer edge. After
all other stitching has been completed,
outline flower centers and work veins in
leaves in couching with color 8.

PEONY

COLOR KEY *for DMC 3-Ply Persian Wool*

1 White
2 Very Dark Moss Green (7034)
3 Dark Cranberry (7601)
4 Baby Pink (7818)
5 DMC Gold Embroidery Thread, Art. 282

DIRECTIONS

Work with one strand of yarn in needle.
Work petals in long and short stitch,
shading from dark at center to light at
outer edge. After all stitching has been
completed, outline petals in couching
with color 5.

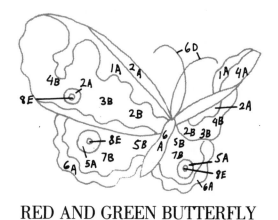

RED AND GREEN BUTTERFLY

ORANGE AND RED
BUTTERFLY

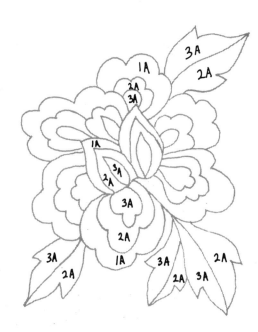

PEONY

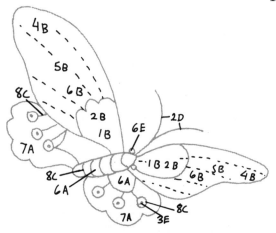

PINK AND YELLOW BUTTERFLY

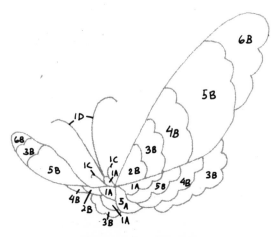

GREEN BUTTERFLY

RED AND GREEN BUTTERFLY

COLOR KEY *for DMC 6-Strand Floss*

1 Garnet Red (816)
2 Medium Coral (350)
3 Light Coral (352)
4 Peach (353)
5 Sky Blue (519)
6 Kelly Green (702)
7 Very Light Loden Green (772)
8 DMC Gold Embroidery Thread, Art. 282

DIRECTIONS

Work with three strands of floss in needle. After all other stitching has been completed, outline body and spots in couching with one strand of color 8. With color 8, take several straight stitches across body and from body to tip of each wing.

STITCH KEY for All Designs

A Satin Stitch
B Long and Short Stitch
C Couching
D Outline Stitch
E French Knot
H Straight Stitch

ORANGE AND RED BUTTERFLY

COLOR KEY *for DMC 6-Strand Floss*

1 Dark Terra-Cotta (3550
2 Black (310)
3 Lemon Yellow (307)
4 Light Coral (352)
5 Burnt Orange (947)
6 DMC Silver Metallic Thread, Art. 281

DIRECTIONS

Work with three strands of floss in needle. After all other stitching has been completed, outline wings and outer edge of antennae in couching with one strand of color 6.

PEONY

COLOR KEY *for DMC Matte Embroidery Cotton*

1 Dark Coral (2349)
2 Very Dark Terra-Cotta (2354)
3 Very Dark Garnet Red (2902)
4 DMC Silver Metallic Thread, Art. 281

DIRECTIONS

Work with one strand of thread in needle. Work each petal in satin stitch, shading from dark at center to light at outer edge. After all other stitching has been completed, outline petals and work center veins of leaves in couching with one strand of color 4.

PINK AND YELLOW BUTTERFLY

COLOR KEY *for DMC Pearl Cotton #5*

1 Light Pistachio Green (368)
2 Medium Pistachio Green (320)
3 Dark Pistachio Green (367)
4 Peach (353)
5 Coral (351)
6 Garnet Red (816)
7 Light Lemon Yellow (445)
8 DMC Gold Embroidery Thread, Art. 282

DIRECTIONS

Work with one strand of thread in needle. After all other stitching has been completed, outline body, spots, wings and antennae in couching with one strand of color 8. Couch lines along wings as indicated by broken lines on chart, using color 8.

GREEN BUTTERFLY

COLOR KEY *for DMC 6-Strand Floss*

1 Garnet Red (816)
2 Peach (353)
3 Very Light Loden Green (772)
4 Bright Chartreuse (704)
5 Kelly Green (702)
6 Sky Blue (519)
7 DMC Silver Embroidery Thread, Art. 283

DIRECTIONS

Work with three strands of floss in needle. After all other stitching has been completed, outline wings and body in couching with one strand of color 7. Couch straight lines across each wing from body to tip of wing with color 7.

Stitch and Color Chart for Plate 24, TWO PHOENIXES

COLOR KEY *for DMC Matte Embroidery Cotton*

1 Royal Blue (2797)
2 Dark Delft Blue (2798)
3 Pale Delft Blue (2800)
4 DMC Gold Metallic Thread, Art. 280

STITCH KEY

A Satin Stitch
C Couching
E French Knot
H Straight Stitch

DIRECTIONS

Work with one strand of thread in needle. The entire design is worked in couching unless otherwise indicated. Each area is worked in three shades of blue. Unmarked areas are worked the same as similar nearby marked areas and the right side of the design is a mirror image of the left side. After all other stitching has been completed, work couching with one strand of color 4 as indicated.